BOOK 3

Current Hits
for Two

**6 Graded Duets for
Late Intermediate Pianists**

Arranged by
...ates

Produced by
Alfred Music
P.O. Box 10003
Van Nuys, CA 91410-0003
alfred.com

Printed in USA.

ISBN-10: 1-4706-2334-X
ISBN-13: 978-1-4706-2334-0

Cover Image
Manhattan night view: © iStockphoto.com / huseyintuncer

BELIEVER

SECONDO

Words and Music by Zachary Barnett,
James Adam Shelley, Matthew Sanchez,
David Rublin, Shep Goodman and Aaron Accetta
Arranged by Dan Coates

BELIEVER
PRIMO

Words and Music by Zachary Barnett,
James Adam Shelley, Matthew Sanchez,
David Rublin, Shep Goodman and Aaron Accetta
Arranged by Dan Coates

SECONDO

SECONDO

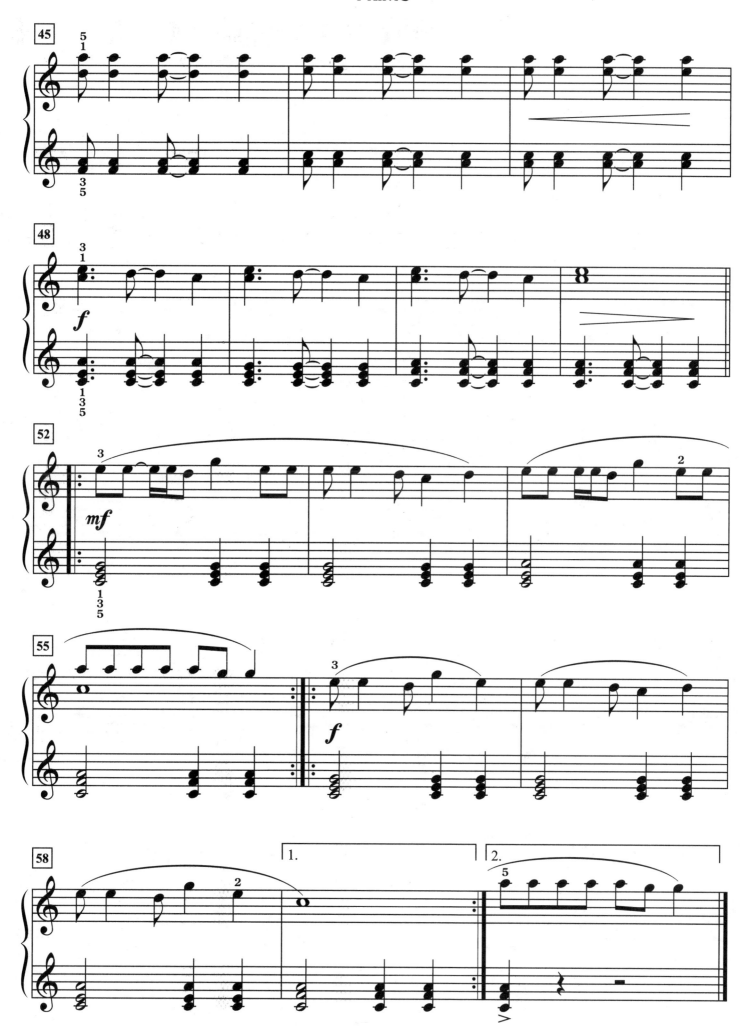

BEST DAY OF MY LIFE

SECONDO

Words and Music by Zachary Barnett,
James Adam Shelley, Matthew Sanchez,
David Rublin, Shep Goodman and Aaron Accetta
Arranged by Dan Coates

BEST DAY OF MY LIFE
PRIMO

Words and Music by Zachary Barnett,
James Adam Shelley, Matthew Sanchez,
David Rublin, Shep Goodman and Aaron Accetta
Arranged by Dan Coates

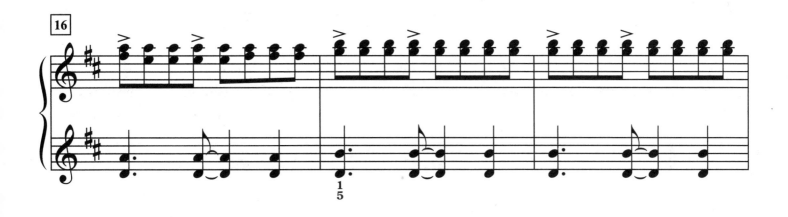

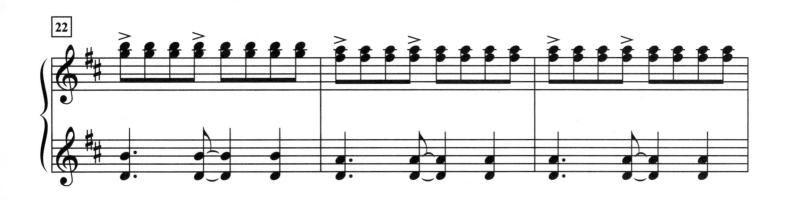

GIRL ON FIRE

SECONDO

Words and Music by Billy Squier,
Jeffrey Bhakser, Alicia Keys and Salaam Remi
Arranged by Dan Coates

GIRL ON FIRE

PRIMO

Words and Music by Billy Squier,
Jeffrey Bhakser, Alicia Keys and Salaam Remi
Arranged by Dan Coates

SECONDO

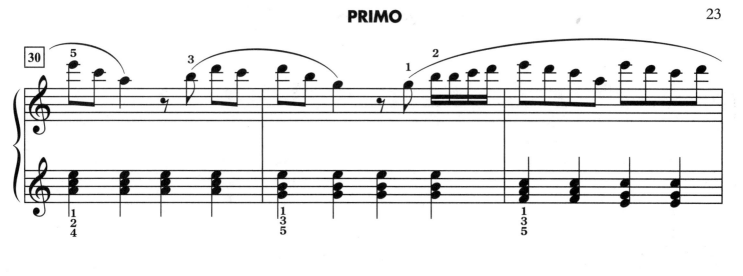

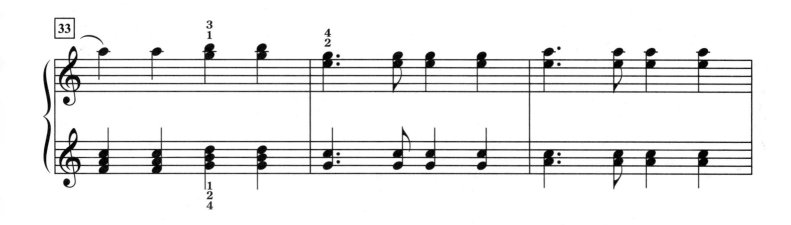

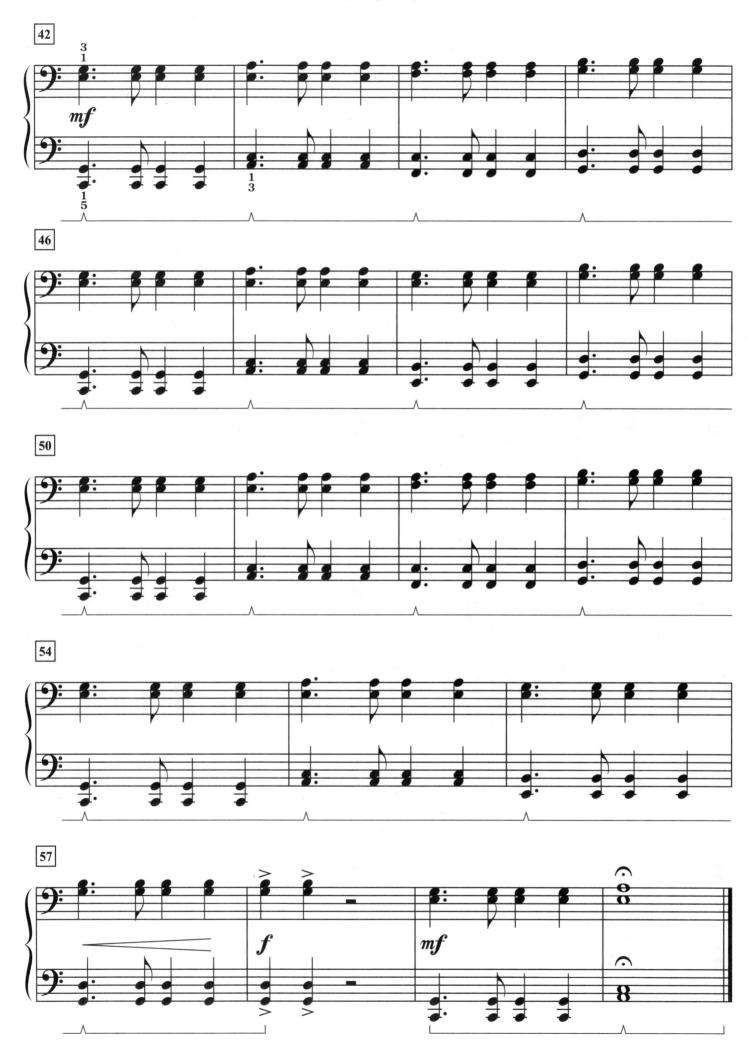

PAYPHONE
SECONDO

Words and Music by Wiz Khalifa,
Adam Levine, Benjamin Levin, Ammar Malik,
Johan Schuster and Daniel Omelio
Arranged by Dan Coates

Moderately bright

PAYPHONE

PRIMO

Words and Music by Wiz Khalifa,
Adam Levine, Benjamin Levin, Ammar Malik,
Johan Schuster and Daniel Omelio
Arranged by Dan Coates

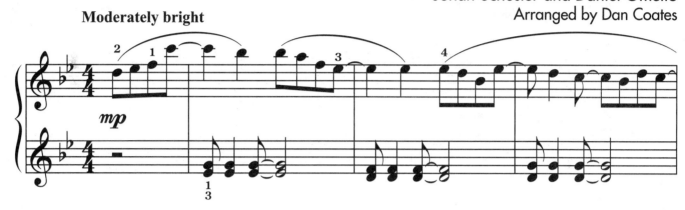

SECONDO

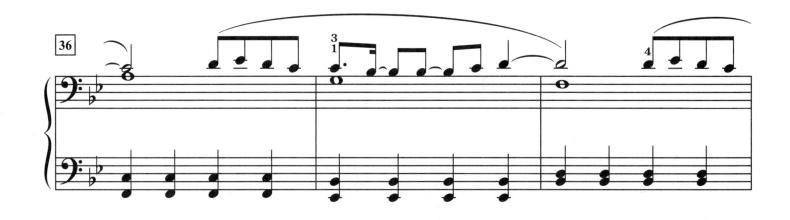

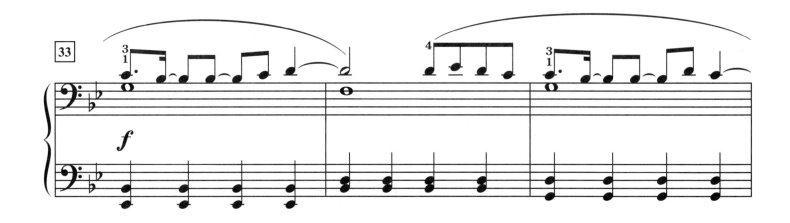

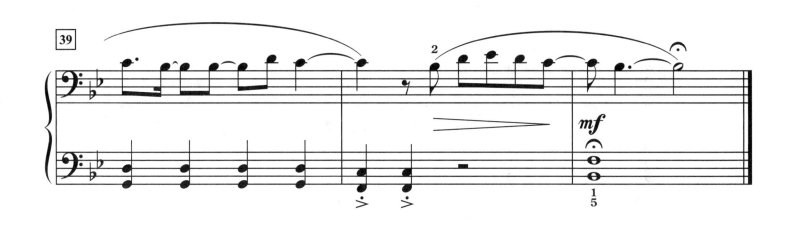

A THOUSAND YEARS

SECONDO

Words and Music by
David Hodges and Christina Perri
Arranged by Dan Coates

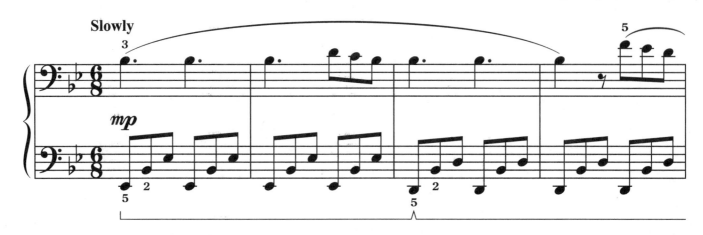

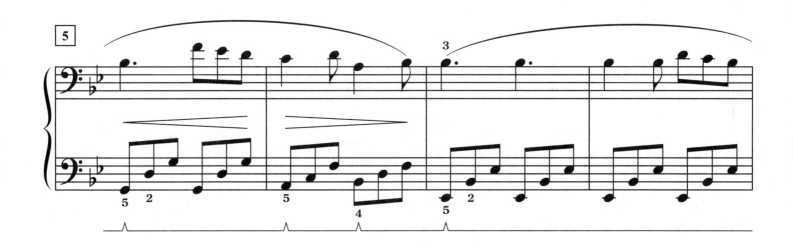

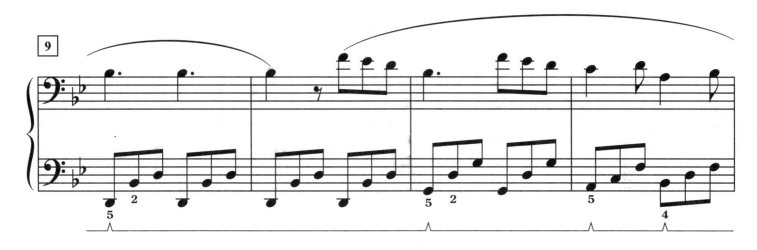

A THOUSAND YEARS

PRIMO

Words and Music by
David Hodges and Christina Perri
Arranged by Dan Coates

SECONDO

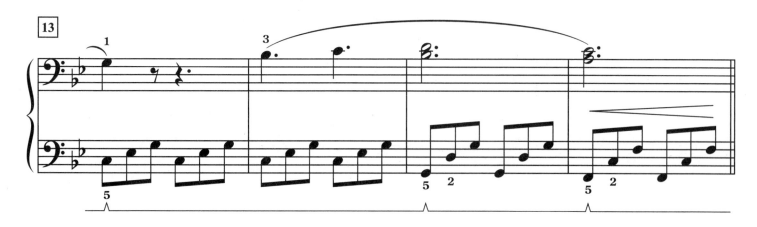

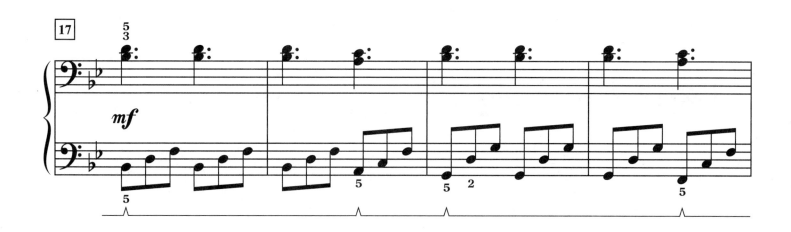

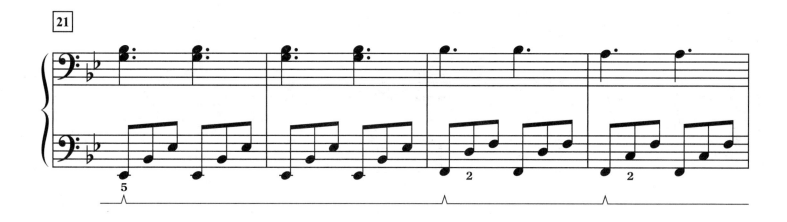

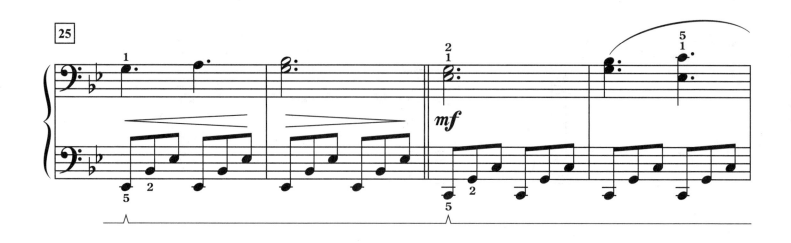

SECONDO

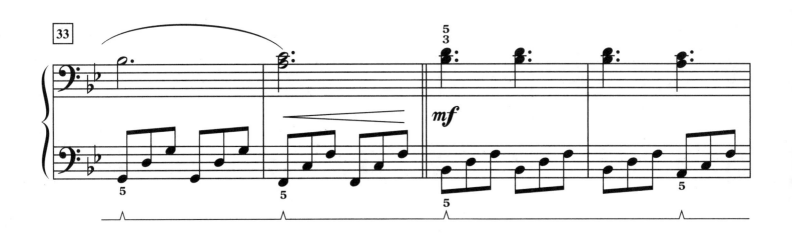

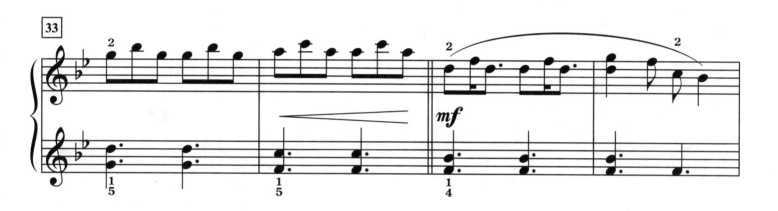

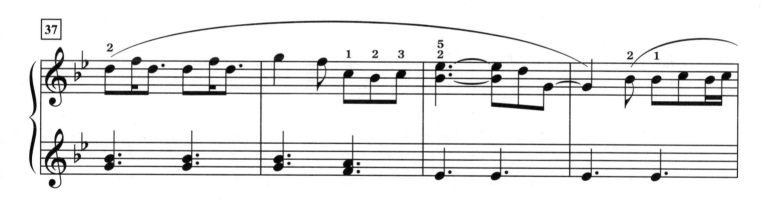

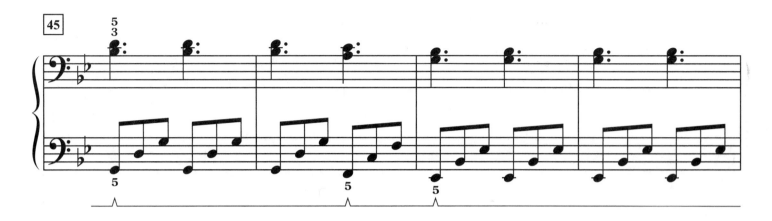

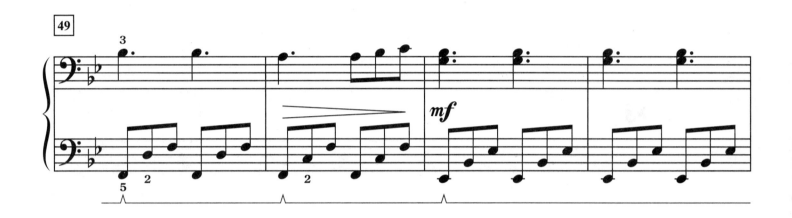

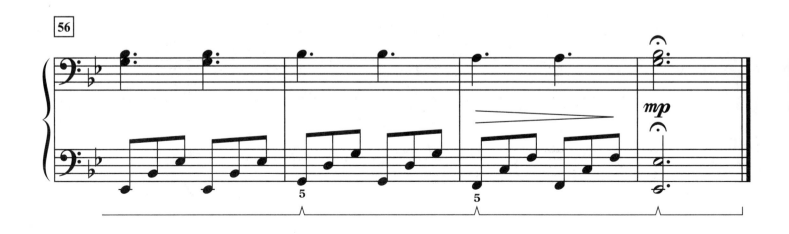

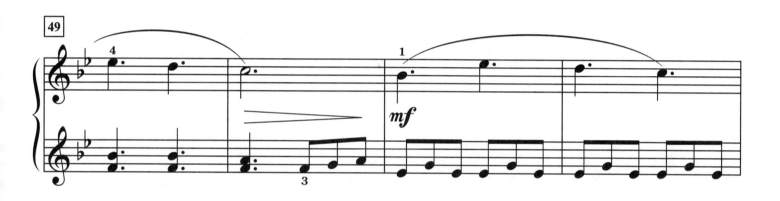

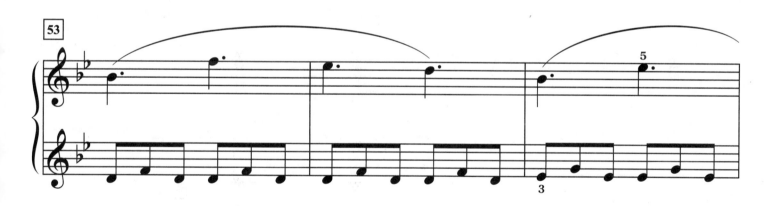

WHEN I WAS YOUR MAN

SECONDO

Words and Music by Philip Lawrence,
Andrew Wyatt, Bruno Mars and Ari Levine
Arranged by Dan Coates

WHEN I WAS YOUR MAN

PRIMO

Words and Music by Philip Lawrence,
Andrew Wyatt, Bruno Mars and Ari Levine
Arranged by Dan Coates

SECONDO

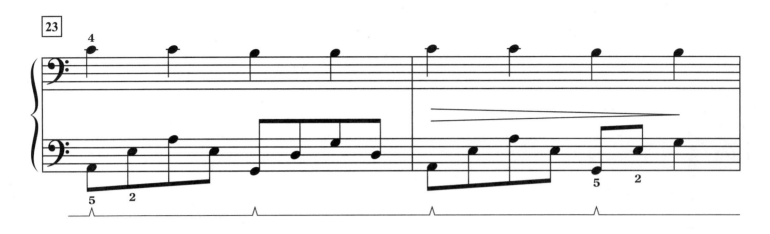

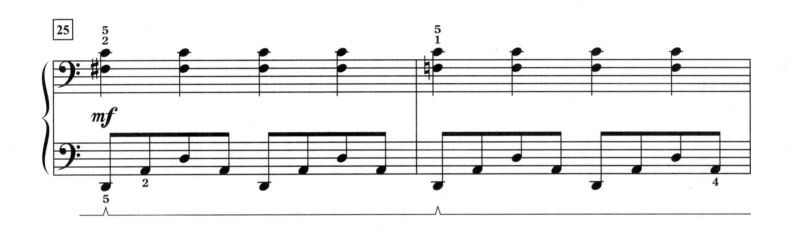

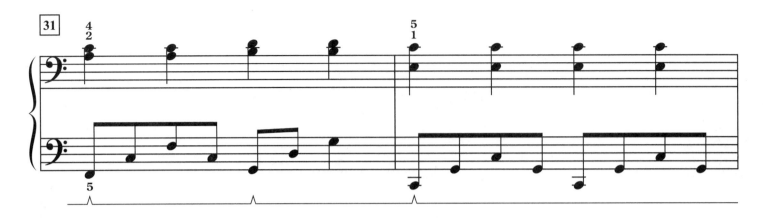

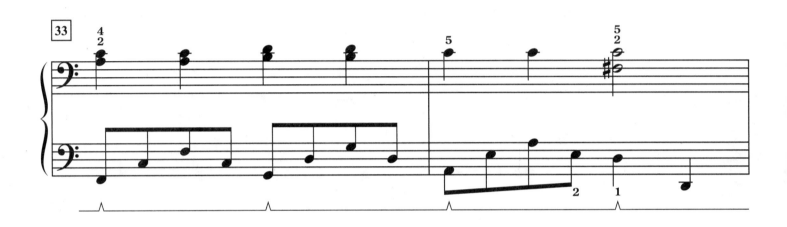

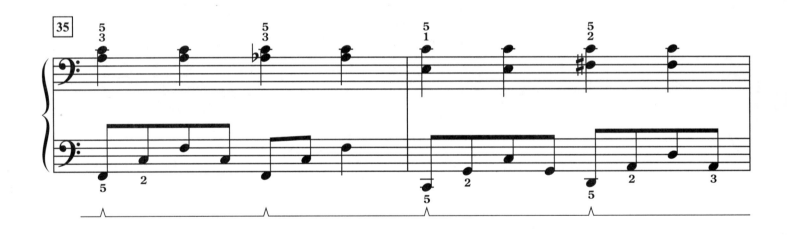

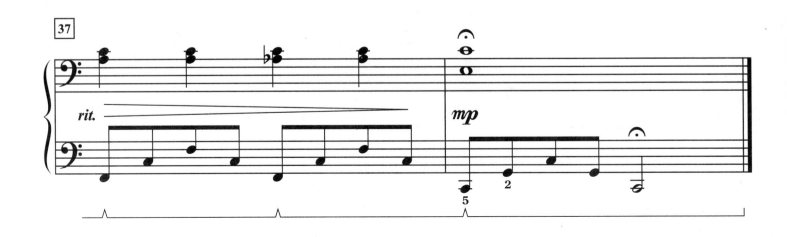

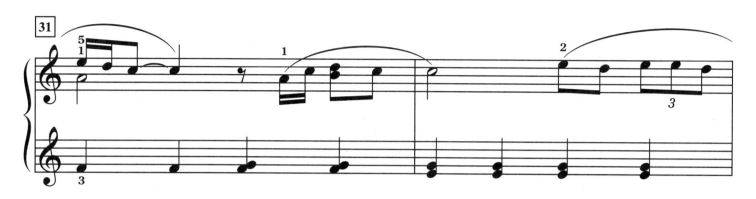

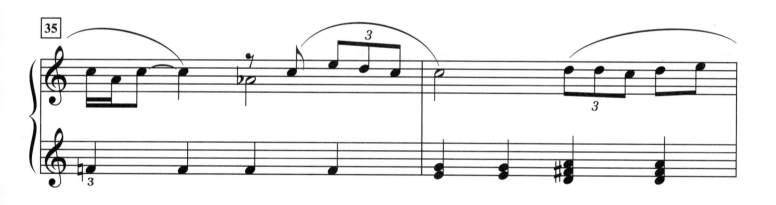

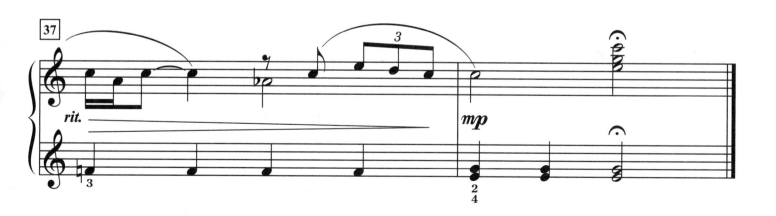